AMERICA'S INDUSTRIAL SOCIETY IN THE 19TH CENTURY ™

The Republican Party in the Late 1800s

A Changing Role for American Government

Bill Stites

rosen central
Primary Source™

The Rosen Publishing Group, Inc., New York

Published in 2004 by The Rosen Publishing Group, Inc.
29 East 21st Street, New York, NY 10010

First Edition

Library of Congress Cataloging-in-Publication Data

Stites, Bill.
The Republican Party in the late 1800s: a changing role for American government/by Bill Stites—1st ed.
    p. cm.—(America's industrial society in the 19th century)
Includes bibliographical references and index.
ISBN 0-8239-4030-6 (library binding)
ISBN 0-8239-4285-6 (paperback)
6-pack ISBN 0-8239-4297-X
1. Republican Party (U.S.: 1854)—History—19th century. 2. United States—Politics and government—19th century.
I. Title. II. Series.
JK2356.S75 2003
324.2734'09'034—dc21

           2002153978

Manufactured in the United States of America

On the cover: first row (from left to right): steamship docked at a landing; Tammany Hall on Election Night, 1859; map showing U.S. railroad routes in 1883; detail of bank note, 1822, Bank of the Commonwealth of Kentucky; People's Party (Populist) Convention at Columbus, Nebraska, 1890; Republican ticket, 1865 (also shown enlarged). Second row (from left to right): William McKinley gives a campaign speech in 1896; parade banner of the Veterans of the Haymarket Riot; Alexander Graham Bell's sketch of the telephone, c. 1876; public declaration of the government's ability to crush monopolies; city planners' illustration of Stockton, California; railroad construction camp, Nebraska, 1889.

Photo credits: cover, p. 21 © Library of Congress, Rare Book and Special Collections Division; pp. 5, 6, 8, 11, 12, 14, 17, 20, 23, 26 © Library of Congress, Prints and Photographs Division; pp. 18, 27 © Bettmann/Corbis.

Series Design: Tahara Hasan; **Editor:** Jill Jarnow

Contents

1
The Perils of Prosperity

The Republican Party formed in 1854 with one goal in mind: The members wanted to abolish slavery. Abraham Lincoln was elected president of the United States in 1860. He was the first Republican president.

Slavery fueled the South. Slaves toiled so that landowners could make money. When Lincoln became president, Southern states seceded from the United States. They formed the Confederate States of America. White slave owners from the South were Democrats.

In 1861, the North and the South went to war with each other. The American Civil War became the bloodiest and most costly war in U.S. history.

When it was over, Republicans got their wish. Slavery was outlawed. The slaves were free. But two weeks after the war ended, Lincoln was killed by an assassin's bullet.

As the sixteenth president, Abraham Lincoln built the Republican Party into a strong national organization. He also urged the Northern Democrats to join the Union in abolishing slavery. On January 1, 1863, Lincoln issued the Emancipation Proclamation, a document which declared the slaves of the Confederacy free forever.

Andrew Johnson was Lincoln's vice president. Now Johnson was president of the United States. Before the war, he had been a Democrat. As president, Johnson could not agree with Congress about anything.

The Republicans wanted black people to be citizens. They wanted to give black men the right to vote. Johnson wouldn't let them. The Republicans wanted the South to pay for the war. Johnson wanted to let go of the past.

Southerners still did not have the right to vote. They had lost it in the war. Johnson did not stand a chance of being reelected.

Ulysses S. Grant won the election in 1868 by a land-slide. He had been the Northern hero of the Civil War. Now he was president of the United States.

This cartoon depicts the Union defeat of the Confederacy. A cannon labeled "Death to Traitors!" is aimed at a monster known as secession. The small demons flying through the air are the states that left the Union. Two undecided states are represented by creatures with two heads.

The Republicans controlled both Congress and the White House. It looked like the slavery conflict was finally over. White Southerners still did not want to give rights to blacks. But with Johnson gone, the government united against them. The South would need to give in eventually. The country could rebuild.

Grant oversaw the rebuilding of the South. One by one, the states were readmitted into the Union. Union soldiers started to come home from the South. And black men were guaranteed the right to vote.

Grant did not show good leadership as president. He had been a much better general. But most people loved Grant anyway. He was still a hero. He was reelected by the Northern states in 1872. He won by an even wider margin than in 1868.

Meanwhile, a curious thing was happening. America was getting rich. Big factories were springing up throughout the Northeast. The railroad ran across the country. Factory owners could use the railroads to carry their goods to new markets. People were discovering gold and oil in the West.

Of course, the people who worked in the factories did not become rich. Neither did the people who built the railroads. But factory and railroad owners became very rich. They were richer than anyone in America had ever been.

The rich had a lot of money to invest. They became even richer. More wealth meant more taxes to collect. Suddenly the government was rich, too. And many politicians believed they deserved a share of this money.

Soon government scandals began piling up. Grant's reputation was destroyed. He was never involved in a scandal. But almost everyone around him was. His vice president accepted bribes from a railroad company. Four cabinet secretaries either stole money or took bribes.

Even worse, his personal secretary stole millions in tax dollars. This was the biggest problem. The secretary was Grant's close friend. Grant tried to get him off the hook. It worked. The secretary did not go to jail. But the public

ARRIVAL OF DELEGATES TO THE REPUBLICAN CONVENTION AT CHICAGO.—Sketched by W. R. Baird.—[See Page 367.]

An illustration depicting the arrival of the delegates to the 1868 Republican National Convention in Chicago. The Republicans nominated Ulysses S. Grant of Illinois to be their candidate for president.

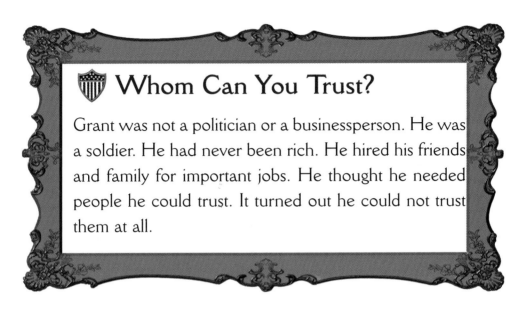

Whom Can You Trust?

Grant was not a politician or a businessperson. He was a soldier. He had never been rich. He hired his friends and family for important jobs. He thought he needed people he could trust. It turned out he could not trust them at all.

was not satisfied. He had to be fired anyway. And it made Grant look like a cheat.

On top of everything, the country plunged into a depression. Rich people lost their money. Companies went out of business. Factories closed. Thousands of people lost their jobs. Then, Congress started handing out huge raises. Grant's salary was doubled. Members of Congress paid themselves much more, too.

The public was furious. People began to call for reform. They wanted the government to play by the rules. Grant decided not to run again in 1876. Even he thought the White House needed someone new. But what happened next made things even worse.

2
A Stolen Election

Grant was out of the picture. The Republicans needed a new candidate. The election was extremely important.

The Southern states could now vote again. Black men could vote, too. But it almost did not matter. Southern whites were still menacing blacks. They kept them from voting. It seemed that the Democrats would win the entire South.

Most of the North would vote Republican. So the election came down to four swing states. They were New York, New Jersey, Ohio, and Indiana. Whoever won those states would win the election.

The Republicans picked a man from Ohio to be their candidate. He was the state's governor, Rutherford B. Hayes. The Republicans hoped that he would assure them victory in Ohio. Hayes was also part of an increasingly rare

Rutherford B. Hayes and William A. Wheeler are portrayed on this Grand National Republican banner for the 1876 Republican presidential campaign. The words "Liberty and Union" appear above the bald eagle. Because of debate over who had won, Hayes was not recognized as president until two days before his inauguration.

breed. He was an honest politician. Like Grant, he was also a war hero. He seemed to be a good man for the job. But the Republicans had a tough fight ahead.

The Republicans traveled the North on the campaign trail. They gave speeches to remind people that the Democrats had seceded from the Union. The Democrats had started the war. They hoped the memory of the war would make people vote Republican. They hoped voters would forget Grant's horrible second term.

An engraving of Ulysses S. Grant by August Hageboeck dated circa 1872. After serving as president, Grant became a partner in a financial firm that went bankrupt. When he learned that he had throat cancer, Grant began to write his life's story in order to pay debts and provide for his family. Soon after finishing the book in 1885, he died. The memoir earned his estate $450,000.

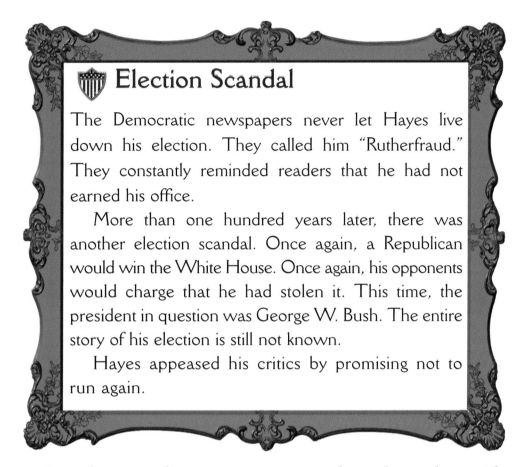

Election Scandal

The Democratic newspapers never let Hayes live down his election. They called him "Rutherfraud." They constantly reminded readers that he had not earned his office.

More than one hundred years later, there was another election scandal. Once again, a Republican would win the White House. Once again, his opponents would charge that he had stolen it. This time, the president in question was George W. Bush. The entire story of his election is still not known.

Hayes appeased his critics by promising not to run again.

On election day, Hayes appeared to have lost. The Democrats had won New York, New Jersey, and Indiana. But the Republicans would not give up. They decided to change the results from three other states.

Their loophole was a law passed under Grant. The law was designed to protect the voting rights of blacks. Congress could throw out election results if even a single black man was prevented from voting.

Hayes had lost the election. But blacks had been stopped from voting. The Democrats had broken the law.

The Republicans focused on Louisiana, Florida, and South Carolina. They could win the election for Hayes. The Republicans just needed to throw out enough votes. They could take those three states for themselves.

Chief Justice Morrison R. Waite administered the oath of office to Rutherford B. Hayes during his inauguration in 1877. They stood on the east portico of the U.S. Capitol. Hayes was the third president to move the ceremony to a Monday because March 4, the traditional day of inauguration, fell on a Sunday. Hayes had taken the oath privately on March 3, 1877.

Hayes was an honest man. He did not know what to do. But he believed the country needed a Republican president. Besides, blacks were being denied their right to vote. Almost every black man who did vote voted Republican. Of course, black voters would support the party that freed them. So why had the states gone Democratic? Because blacks were being kept away. That was not right. But was it right to steal the election?

The parties struck a deal two days before the inauguration. Hayes would be president. The Democrats gave in. But the Republicans had to give up something, too. They had to remove all remaining soldiers from the South. And they could not enforce the civil rights laws there.

The Republicans won the White House. But the Southerners got their way. Black people in the South had essentially lost their rights. And they would not get them back for nearly eighty years.

Hayes proved himself to be an honest president. He worked to reform the government. He fired many corrupt officials. But he did not seek reelection in 1880. The election scandal had been too upsetting for him.

3
Welcome to the Machine

As the 1880 election drew near, the Republicans were under a lot of pressure. They could not steal the White House again. This time they needed to win honestly. They knew the Southern states would vote for the Democrats. To win, the Republicans needed to take all four swing states.

Republicans picked another man from Ohio to be their presidential candidate. He was a popular congressman named James Garfield. They hoped he could lock up one swing state.

In the last election, the Republicans had run a New Yorker for vice president. And they had still lost the state. They needed a person from New York who could win. So they turned to the state's party machine.

A Republican campaign poster for the presidential election of 1880 is headed "Our Nation's Choice." It shows General James Abram Garfield, candidate for president and General Chester A. Arthur, candidate for vice president. Garfield and Arthur campaigned for veteran pensions, railroad and corporation grants, and unrestricted Chinese immigration.

OUR NATION'S CHOICE.

HARMONY, PEACE AND PROSPERITY.

OUR NATION'S HONOR WILL BE PRESERVED.

Gen. JAMES ABRAM GARFIELD,
Republican Candidate for President.

Gen. CHESTER A. ARTHUR,
Republican Candidate for Vice-President.

THE PLATFORM OF THE REPUBLICAN PARTY, ADOPTED AT THE Convention in Chicago, JUNE 2-8, 1880.

DEVOTION TO THE UNION.

PUBLISHED BY HAASIS & LUBRECHT, 44 VESEY ST. NEW YORK.

AGENTS WANTED.

Party machines were another peculiar result of America's new wealth. For one thing, more factories meant more jobs. More jobs meant more immigrants coming to the United States every year. Immigrants were usually desperate. They needed jobs. They worked hard in factories. They wanted to become citizens. Soon, the parties figured something out. By helping immigrants, they created loyal party supporters.

Loyalty was very important to the machines. The parties also required loyalty of government workers. Every worker had to give the party part of his salary.

Before long, the machines were huge, rich organizations. They controlled every aspect of life in the big cities.

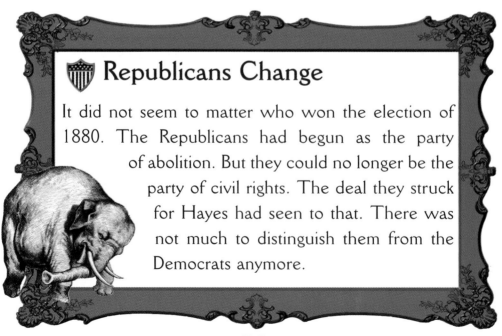

Republicans Change

It did not seem to matter who won the election of 1880. The Republicans had begun as the party of abolition. But they could no longer be the party of civil rights. The deal they struck for Hayes had seen to that. There was not much to distinguish them from the Democrats anymore.

Whatever you needed, the machine could get it for you. But you had to give something back. Usually, the party wanted money. Money made the machines corrupt. They used it to buy elections.

Party machines were the most powerful in New York. They were more powerful than the government. They were also very corrupt. They stole millions of dollars from business and the government. President Hayes tried to reform the machines. He tried to put an end to the corruption. He fired many machine members.

But the Republicans needed to win New York in 1880. And they knew only the machine could do it for them. So they picked one of the men Hayes had fired. They nominated Chester A. Arthur to be vice president.

Garfield and Arthur won the election. They carried all four swing states. They did not need to cheat. They let the machines cheat for them. And they still barely won the popular election.

Garfield was not president for long. Three months after he took office, he was shot. His murderer was a machine politician who wanted a job. Garfield would not give him one, so he took his revenge.

The public could not believe Chester Arthur was their new president. At that time, the country desperately

needed reform. And now it had a corrupt machine politician for president.

But Arthur, like Hayes before him, surprised people. He no longer answered to the machine. Arthur did more for reform than Hayes had. He did what Grant would not do.

President Garfield was in office two hundred days when Charles Guiteau gunned him down on July 2, 1881. An illustration titled "The Attack on the President's Life" appeared in *Frank Leslie's Illustrated Newspaper* on July 16, 1881. It shows the scene in the ladies' room of the Baltimore and Ohio Railroad depot as the assassin was arrested.

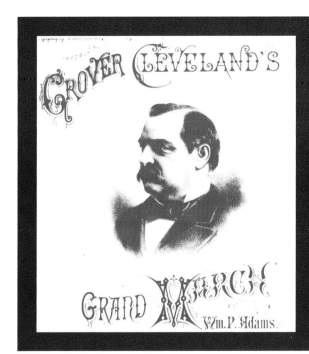

The musical score *Grover Cleveland's Grand March* honored the Democratic Party's candidate with an inscription on the cover that says, "Respectfully dedicated to his excellency Gov. Cleveland of New York, the Democratic nominee for president." During Cleveland's term, he supported the installation of the Statue of Liberty and continued to reform civil service.

He fired and prosecuted a corrupt friend. He became very popular. But he angered the machine, which did not want change. They refused to nominate him again in 1884.

The public did not want a Republican if the candidate was not Arthur. Instead, they elected an honest, unknown Democrat from New York. His name was Grover Cleveland. He was the first Democrat to be elected president since before the Civil War.

4
A Failed Presidency

The machine ruined Cleveland's presidency, too. This time it was the Democratic machine. In New York, the Democratic machine was called Tammany Hall. It was the most powerful and corrupt in the country.

Cleveland was a Democrat from New York. But he had never been part of Tammany Hall. He stood up to Tammany Hall. That was exactly why New Yorkers liked him.

When the Democrats chose him for president, Tammany Hall got mad. They told immigrants in New York to vote Republican. To them, Cleveland was worse than a Republican. They refused to support a Democratic president they had not picked.

But this time, the immigrants did not listen to Tammany Hall. Days before the election, a Republican priest angered them. He gave a racist speech mocking the Irish. The Irish were so angry they ignored Tammany Hall.

This portrait of William Marcy Tweed, known as Boss Tweed, appeared on a tobacco label in 1869. The Tweed Ring stole between thirty and two hundred million dollars from New York City between 1865 and 1871. They controlled all Democratic nominations in New York, using illegal methods to help their candidates win.

They voted for Cleveland. His own party had tried to stop him. Cleveland won. But Tammany Hall would not forget.

In 1888, Tammany Hall tried to stop Cleveland's election once again. This time it worked. The Republicans picked another candidate from a swing state. The state was Indiana. The man was Benjamin Harrison. The Republicans worked hard to turn the Irish against Cleveland. Both parties were working against him. Cleveland's days in the White House were numbered. He won the popular vote. But he lost in the electoral college. The Republicans were back in the White House.

Harrison looked like the right person for the job. He had fought in the Civil War just like Garfield, Grant, and Hayes. His grandfather, William Henry Harrison, had already been president. His great-grandfather had signed the Declaration of Independence.

The American people chose Cleveland in the popular vote. But the electoral college gave them Harrison. Voters had not chosen Chester Arthur either. But he had managed to win their trust. Harrison would not do the same.

Early in his term, Harrison imposed the McKinley tariff. It was the highest tariff the country had ever seen. It made goods more expensive. This angered the middle class. In 1890, the Republicans lost control of Congress.

The economy got worse. People lost their jobs. Stock prices fell. People missed President Cleveland. Under him, things had been stable. Now things were bad and getting worse. People blamed Harrison.

In 1892, the Democrats saw a chance for victory. They nominated Cleveland again. He took New York this time. He won back the White House.

5
A Party Reborn

Cleveland did not make things better. He sided with business, hurting workers. America's economic policies caused a gold crisis. The stock market was depressed. More people were out of work than ever before. Cleveland did not know what to do about it.

Many people felt the answer was imperialism. They thought the United States needed to expand into other lands. Conquered countries would provide the United States with new resources and markets. Cleveland refused.

In 1894, railroad workers in Chicago went on strike. They demanded better treatment and better pay. Cleveland sent federal troops to break the strike. The strike organizer was sent to prison with no trial. People were outraged. The Democrats did not nominate Cleveland again in 1896.

Ten years earlier, President Harrison had passed high tariff laws. People hated them. But now, the Republicans

The Pullman Strike of 1894, which took place in Chicago, was the first national strike in the United States. It involved 150,000 people in twenty-seven states and territories. To end the strike, President Cleveland sent in federal troops against the wishes of Governor Altgeld of Illinois, another United States first. In this photo, an impoverished laborer lives in a shanty town in Chicago during the strike.

decided Harrison had been right. For president, they nominated the man behind Harrison's tariff. His name was William McKinley. The election was split among several parties. But McKinley still won. A Republican had not been fairly elected president since Grant.

Republican campaign buttons from 1900 show Thomas McKinley, candidate for president, and Theodore Roosevelt, candidate for vice president. As the twenty-fifth president of the United States, McKinley focused on foreign policy. He gained control of the Philippines, Guam, and Puerto Rico after the Hundred Days' War with Spain.

McKinley entered the White House in the spring of 1897. The economy improved. Stock prices rose and unemployment fell. McKinley believed in imperialism. He did what Cleveland would not do. He took over Hawaii. The American empire had begun.

Grateful Americans started calling the Republicans the Grand Old Party. They are still called the GOP today. After years of conflict, the Republicans were more popular than ever.

Forty years before, the Republican Party was a single-issue third party. But the Republicans had elected seven of the last eight presidents. Their renewed popularity would last well into the next century. Five of the next six presidents would be Republicans, too.

Glossary

abolish (**uh-BAH-lish**)   To do away with.

candidate (**KAN-dih-dayt**)   One who runs in an election.

corrupt (**kuh-RUPT**)   Crooked. Willing to steal for personal gain.

electoral college (**ih-LEK-tuh-rul KAH-lihj**)   A group of people who elect the president. Each state has a specific number of electoral votes. The decision of the electoral college is based on who won the most electoral votes. A candidate can win the popular vote but still lose in the electoral college and the election.

imperialism (**im-PEER-ee-uhl-ih-zum**)   The process of a country taking over other lands. Usually done for economic reasons.

inauguration (**ih-naw-gyuh-RAY-shun**)   The event of swearing in a government official.

nominate (**NAH-mih-nayt**)   To suggest that someone or something should be given an award or a position.

party machines (**PAR-tee mah-SHEENZ**)   The huge, corrupt political organizations that arose in the big cities.

perils (**PEH-rilz**)   Dangers.

popular vote (**PAH-pyoo-lar VOHT**)   The total number of votes cast nationwide.

prosperity (**prah-SPEHR-ih-tee**)   The condition of being successful. Often refers to money.

reform (**rih-FORM**)   The process of eliminating corruption and strengthening the law.

secede (**sih-SEED**)   To withdraw from a group or a country.

strike (**STRYK**)   A refusal to work until changes are made.

swing states (**SWING STAYTZ**)   States whose populations are torn between the two political parties. States that could swing either way in an election.

tariff (**TAR-iff**)   A tax placed on goods imported from other countries. It supports U.S. businesses by making foreign goods very expensive.

Web Sites

Due to the changing nature of Internet links, the Rosen Publishing Group, Inc., has developed an online list of Web sites related to the subject of this book. This site is updated regularly. Please use this link to access the list:

http://www.rosenlinks.com/aistc/rple

Primary Source Image List

Page 5: A portrait of Abraham Lincoln circa 1846 by Nicholas H. Shepard, now housed at the Library of Congress Prints and Photographs Division in Washington, D.C. Robert Lincoln, the president's son, thought the photograph was taken in either St. Louis or Washington during his father's term in Congress.

Page 6: This political cartoon, titled "Secession Exploded," by William Wiswell was published in Cincinnati on June 18, 1861, and is now housed at the Library of Congress Prints and Photographs Division in Washington, D.C.

Page 8: Currently housed at the Library of Congress Prints and Photographs Division in Washington, D.C., this sketch on a wood engraving by W. B. Baird first appeared in the June 6, 1868, issue of *Harper's Weekly*.

Page 11: Located at the Library of Congress Prints and Photographs Division in Washington, D.C., this banner for the 1876 Republican presidential ticket was published by Currier & Ives.

Page 12: This engraving of Ulysses S. Grant by August Hageboeck dates circa 1872 and is located at the Library of Congress Prints and Photographs Division in Washington, D.C.

Page 14: This photograph, created by the Brady National Photographic Art Gallery in Washington, D.C., was taken in 1877 during the inauguration ceremony of Rutherford B. Hayes at the U.S. Capitol. It is now located at the Library of Congress Prints and Photographs Division in Washington, D.C.

Page 17: This campaign poster for the Republican candidates in the presidential election of 1880 is titled "Our Nation's Choice" and shows portraits of General James Abram Garfield and General Chester A. Arthur. It was published circa 1880 by Haasis & Lubrecht in New York and is now located at the Library of Congress Prints and Photographs Division in Washington, D.C.

Page 18: The elephant symbol of the Republican Party first appeared in *Harper's Weekly* in the November 7, 1874, issue as a part of a political cartoon drawn by cartoonist Thomas Nast. This cartoon was published in the *New York Herald* and shows the Republican vote ready to collapse.

Page 20: This illustration, titled "The Attack on the President's Life" and drawn by A. Berghaus and C. Upham, depicts a scene in the ladies' room of the Baltimore and Ohio Railroad depot after the assassination of President Garfield. This illustration appeared in *Frank Leslie's Illustrated Newspaper* on July 16, 1881. The sketch is housed at the Library of Congress Prints and Photographs Division in Washington, D.C.

Page 21: William P. Adams composed the musical score titled *Grover Cleveland's Grand March* in 1884 for the presidential election of that year. It is now part of the Library of Congress Music Division.

Page 23: This photographic print titled "Our Boss" is of a tobacco label showing a portrait of Boss Tweed and dates circa November 27, 1869. This print is now part of the Library of Congress Prints and Photographs Division in Washington, D.C.

Page 26: A photograph by Ray Stannard Baker taken during the Pullman Labor Strike in 1894. Provided by Corbis.

Page 27: This campaign button for the presidential election of 1900 shows Thomas McKinley for president and Theodore Roosevelt for vice president.

Index

About the Author

Bill Stites is a musician, writer, and teacher living in Brooklyn, New York.